BR TRACTION IN COLOUR

With the morning sun having dispersed the majority of the overnight frost, Birmingham RC&W Class 33/0 No 33027 *Earl Mountbatten of Burma* makes a most attractive picture hauling the 11.17 Milford Haven-Swansea train between Clynderwen and Whitland on 12 January 1985 and is about to pass under the Llandewi to Llanfallteg road.
Nigel Dykhoff

Below:
Clearly labelled 'ScotRail', but in fact sporting InterCity Sector livery, Class 47/4 No 47643 arrives at Dalwhinnie on 1 July 1986 heading the 16.25 Glasgow Queen Street-Inverness train. *Bill Sharman*

Front cover:
No 47484 *Isambard Kingdom Brunel* stands at Penzance on 2 July 1985 with the 10.50 departure to Paddington.
S. Widdowson

Back cover, top:
Class 150/1 'Sprinter' No 150107 and Class 142 'Pacer' No 142034 approach Llandudno Junction on 19 August 1986, forming the 10.42 Manchester-Holyhead.
Mrs D. A. Robinson

Back cover, bottom:
Power car No 43177 leads the InterCity 125 set forming the 12.40 Paddington-Plymouth at Cockwood Harbour on 11 September 1985. *Peter W. Durham*

BR TRACTION IN COLOUR

First published 1987

ISBN 0 7110 1699 2

All rights reserved. No part of this book may be reproduced or transmitted in any form or by any means, electronic or mechanical, including photo- copying, recording or by any information storage and retrieval system, without permission from the Publisher in writing.

© Ian Allan Ltd 1987

Published by Ian Allan Ltd, Shepperton, Surrey; and printed by Ian Allan Printing Ltd at their works at Coombelands in Runnymede, England

Below:
Western Region Class 142 'Skipper' DMU No 142023 is pictured near Lympstone on 15 July 1986 forming the 13.45 train from Exmouth to Exeter St Davids. *Brian Morrison*

Below right:
Although Ripple Lane depot has no official allocation of its own, it rarely contains less than a dozen locomotives and, at weekends, many more. On a sunny 18 November 1979, some of the locomotives present are Class 47/0s Nos 47116, 47016 and 47085 *Mammoth* **and Class 31/1s Nos 31143 and 31175.**
Brian Morrison

CONTENTS

A Class 254 InterCity 125 led by power car No 43065 races through Pilmoor on 9 August 1986, forming the 13.00 King's Cross-Aberdeen service. *John E. Oxley*

ONE

INTERCITY AND INTER-REGIONAL

British Rail's InterCity network radiates from Paddington to Bristol, Wales and the West Country; from Euston to Birmingham, Manchester, Liverpool, Glasgow and Inverness; from King's Cross to Hull, Leeds, Newcastle, Edinburgh and Aberdeen; from St Pancras to Nottingham, Derby and Sheffield; from Liverpool Street to East Anglia, and also incorporates North-east/South-west route trains via both Birmingham New Street and Kensington Olympia in London. With the exception of trains from Euston, some from Paddington and Liverpool Street and the cross-London services, motive power is usually entrusted to the InterCity 125 High Speed Trains. Electric locomotives, primarily of Classes 86 and 87, work the West Coast main line expresses and Class 86s some of the Liverpool Street ones. Class 47s still appear on some InterCity services from Liverpool Street and Paddington and Class 50s operate extensively on the Western Region, in particular west of Plymouth.

The Inter-Regional cross-country services via Birmingham also utilise some InterCity 125 sets but most of this traffic is still locomotive-hauled, with Classes 47 and 50 now dominating following the withdrawal of large numbers of the Class 45 'Peaks'. The requirement for passengers to change trains on long journeys is very much reduced with through services from Aberdeen and Glasgow to the West Country; from Dundee and Glasgow to Poole; from Liverpool, Manchester, Derby and Wolverhampton to Brighton; from Cardiff to Newcastle; from Liverpool and Manchester to Plymouth and Dover and many more.

Below:
Reflected in the still waters of the Kennet & Avon Canal, near Crofton, a Class 253 HST set, with power car No 43174 leading, heads eastwards along the Berks & Hants route, forming the 07.25 Penzance-Paddington express on 16 June 1984. *John Vaughan*

Top:
Passing the disused signalbox which marks the site of the once busy Brent station in South Devon, Class 50 No 50049 *Defiance* powers the 13.40 Paddington-Penzance towards Plymouth on 16 July 1985.   *Brian Morrison*

Above:
Having arrived with the 08.02 from Glasgow Central, Class 370 Advanced Passenger Train formation No 370007 rests alongside newly-named Class 86/2 electric locomotive No 86245 *Dudley Castle* on the 13.40 to Wolverhampton at Euston on 17 August 1984.   *Brian Morrison*

Right:
With power car number 43187 neatly lettered on the drawbar cover plate, a Class 253 HST set passes Ambergate on 6 July 1985 forming the 16.00 Sheffield-St Pancras service.   *Les Nixon*

DY
564
InterCity125
43187

Right:

When this photograph was taken on 6 July 1979, some two years were to elapse before the revised Class 50 fleet livery of wrap-round yellow ends, black window surrounds, grey roof panels together with large BR logo and TOPS number was to emerge from the BREL Works at Doncaster. In original, albeit work-stained livery, No 50023 *Howe* passes the time-worn but classic setting of Horse Cove, near Dawlish, heading the 11.30 Paddington-Penzance, the renowned 'Cornish Riviera' express. *Brian Morrison*

Below:

On 15 August 1986, the 16.45 Euston-Blackpool North 'Lancashire Pullman' approaches Watford Junction headed by Class 86/2 No 86227 *Sir Henry Johnson*. *John E. Oxley*

Top:
With semaphore signals still extant, Class 47/4 No 47480 *Robin Hood* enters Wellington station on 10 June 1985 rostered to the 11.40 Shrewsbury-Euston service. An electric locomotive will take over from the 'Duff' at Wolverhampton for the remainder of the journey under the wires to London. *Brian J. Robbins*

Above:
Class 50 No 50037 *Illustrious* leaves Cheltenham on the bitterly cold 15 February 1985 with the 09.36 Liverpool Lime Street-Penzance service. *Peter W. Durham*

Right:
With the early morning sun soon to be obliterated by the storm clouds rolling in from the west, a Class 253 HST set, led by power car No 43124, approaches Taunton station on 28 March 1985 forming the 07.25 express from Plymouth to Paddington. *Colin J. Marsden*

Left:

In immaculate InterCity red and grey livery on the day that the locomotive was named *University of London* by Her Royal Highness Princess Anne at Euston station, No 86434 prepares to move away from Euston with the 14.05 for Birmingham New Street on 10 April 1986. *Brian Morrison*

Below:

On 29 May 1985, the down 'Manchester Pullman' races past Slindon, north of Norton Bridge in Staffordshire, hauled by Class 86/1 No 86102 *Robert A. Riddles*. This electric locomotive is just one of a sub-class of three rebuilt with Class 87-type bogies and motors for evaluation of equipment, prior to its installation in the Class 87 fleet. *Hugh Ballantyne*

Bottom:

Class 45/1 'Peak' No 45139 is rostered for the 07.50 Bristol Temple Meads-Penzance service on 5 July 1984 and restarts the train from the scheduled Lostwithiel stop. The line in the foreground is the start of the old Fowey branch, now used for china clay traffic to and from Carne Point. *Brian Morrison*

The time-honoured Liverpool Street setting where everything from early steam engines through to the 'Britannia' Pacifics and, latterly, Class 37 and 47 diesels have been photographed. Now it is the turn of the electric locomotives, with Class 86/2 No 86221 *Vesta* awaiting departure time with the 13.30 to Norwich on 29 May 1985. *Roger Norman*

Below:

Near Glenmuckloch Hall, between New Cumnock and Kirkconnel, on 6 July 1985, Class 47/4 No 47403 *The Geordie* growls past hauling the Saturdays 11.00 Ayr-Euston service. Note the Gateshead depot sticker between the marker lights. *Peter J. Robinson*

Above:
Named Class 254 InterCity 125 power car No 43100 *Craigentinny* leads an immaculate eight-car formation at Plawsworth, Co Durham, on 1 May 1986 forming the 13.35 Edinburgh-King's Cross express. *Peter J. Robinson*

Right:
A scene from the late 1970s as a Class 46 1Co-Co1 No 46043 nears Batley hauling the 07.42 inter-regional service from Newcastle to Liverpool Lime Street. *Gavin Morrison*

TWO

LONDON & SOUTH EAST AND PROVINCIAL

Whilst the High Speed Trains operating the prestigious InterCity services provide most of British Rail's glamour, and are the focus for the majority of their media marketing, it is still the much maligned, taken for granted, traditional train that makes up the largest proportion of timetabled services.

The Network SouthEast area embraces the whole of the Southern Region passenger network and also includes the suburban trains that emanate from the London termini of the Eastern, London Midland and Western Regions. Other than non-passenger workings, the Provincial Sector covers just about everything else and stretches from Wick and Thurso, on the northerly tip of Scotland, to the furthest extremity of Cornwall at Penzance.

Below:
The 09.00 Exeter St Davids-Exmouth local working departs from Exeter Central on 23 July 1985 formed of a Birmingham RC&W Suburban 3-car Class 118 DMU, led by motor brake second No W51303. Observe the colourful graffiti adorning the brickwork of the old signalbox in lieu of the nameplate. *Brian Morrison*

Left:
Class 37 Co-Co No 37237 makes a rousing start from Carlisle with the 14.30 summer Saturdays only Morecambe-Glasgow Central train on a very wet August day in 1978. If the weather in Morecambe was the same as in Carlisle, the returning holidaymakers will be glad to have gone home!
Antony Guppy

Below:
A Cravens Class 105 2-car DMU with driving trailer composite No E54447 leading approaches Spital Bridge, Peterborough, on 24 April 1985 forming the 15.15 service from Birmingham New Street to Cambridge, a journey time of over 3½ hours. *Bill Sharman*

Right:
Resplendent in freshly applied ScotRail livery, Class 47/7 No 47701 *Saint Andrew* leads Class 33/0 No 33035 on the 11.15 Crewe-Bangor train on 19 March 1986 and passes the battlements of the magnificent Conwy Castle. The leading machine is probably on a running-in turn following overhaul at Crewe Works. *Larry Goddard*

Left:
With Class 37s having taken over from the Class 25s on the Cambrian lines from 1985, Nos 37227 and 37220 leave Shrewsbury behind on 18 August 1985 hauling the 07.30 Euston-Aberystwyth summer Saturdays train.
Brian J. Robbins

Below left:
Class 205/1 diesel electric multiple-unit No 1111 was selected for extensive refurbishing during 1979 and emerged from Eastleigh Works in 1980 with gangways fitted, compartments replaced by open seating layout, fluorescent lighting and a public address system. The 3-car unit has since been used extensively on the Ashford-Hastings route where it was photographed on 13 April 1985 arriving at Appledore, Kent, as the 16.40 ex-Ashford.
Brian Morrison

Above:

A slight delay in departure of the 12.25 local service to Morpeth was fortuitous for the photographer on 29 May 1980 when the 12.30 for South Shields left at the same time and brought about this well-positioned view which also includes Class 31/1 No 31139 working light engine. The two Cravens Class 105 2-car DMUs are led by driving trailer composites Nos E56426 and E56459 (latterly Nos 54426 and 54459) and the scene is, of course, the well known one from above Newcastle station. *Brian Morrison*

Right:

A Class 101 Metro-Cammell 2-car DMU, led by driving trailer second No E54071, forms the 10.15 Newcastle-Middlesbrough service at Stockton on 20 August 1984.
Bill Sharman

Top:
Although Four Oaks station lies on the cross-city route from Redditch to Lichfield City, via Birmingham New Street, a number of the services in fact terminate there, resulting in the sidings being used as a stabling point for a number of DMUs. Awaiting their next scheduled duty on 1 March 1984 are two BR Derby-built Class 116 units with the motor brake second cars Nos M53852 and M53062 facing the camera. *Brian Morrison*

Above:
On 6 July 1985 the local passenger service from Tunbridge Wells Central to Eridge via Tunbridge Wells West and Groombridge was withdrawn. Trains were generally formed of St Leonards-based Class 207 diesel electric multiple-units (DEMUs) such as No 1305 pictured here at the impressive Tunbridge Wells West station on 24 April 1985 as the 14.47 from Eridge to Tunbridge Wells Central.
Brian Morrison

Right:
A journey time of over 4½ hours would be in prospect for anyone contemplating travelling the whole route of the 14.20 from Crewe to Cleethorpes. A few passengers alight from the train at Spondon but they have only made a six minute trip from Derby in the Swindon Class 120 3-car DMU No 509. Motor brake second No M53657 is the car nearest to the camera. *Brian Morrison*

BR Derby Class 116 DMU No C335, with motor brake second No W51140 leading, leaves Abercynon on 29 August 1985 forming a Merthyr Tydfil-Cardiff Central train. Note the Welsh Dragon embellishment below the centre cab window. *Les Nixon*

Above left:
With the West Midlands PTE logo prominent on the yellow front, a Class 116 Derby-built DMU, with motor brake second No M53055 leading, leaves Shrewsbury on 6 July 1985 forming the 08.20 to Wolverhampton. On the right, Class 37 No 37294 waits for the road with the delayed 07.53 for Aberystwyth, having arrived earlier as empty coaching stock from Bescot. *John Vaughan*

Left:
A particularly attractive scene at Lincoln on 21 August 1984 with swans in the foreground and the cathedral in the background. A BR Swindon Class 120 Cross-Country DMU makes the crossing of the River Witham at Lincoln St Marks. *Bill Sharman*

Top:
Transferred from the Cardiff 'Valley Lines' allocation to Plymouth Laira to work Cornish branch lines, Pressed Steel Co Class 121 single car 'Bubble' No 55033 still retains the Welsh Dragon emblem at Liskeard on 1 October 1985 whilst working the Looe branch. *Brian Morrison*

Above:
The slab-sided design of the Class 201/202/203 'Hastings' DEMUs was necessary in view of the restricted tunnels on the Hastings route from Tonbridge. It was unusual for these types to operate anywhere other than on the Charing Cross/Cannon Street-Hastings route and in this view Class 201 unit No 1003 approaches Stonegate station on 21 March 1986 forming the 11.45 Charing Cross-Hastings. With the tunnel problems alleviated, the 29-year reign of these units came to an end when the Queen Mother inaugurated the new route electrification that came into full use on 6 May 1986. *Brian Morrison*

Above:
Class 150/1 'Sprinter' unit No 150136 calls at Lowdham station on 10 February 1986, forming the 12.32 Lincoln-Crewe train.
E. A. J. Saunders

Right:
With the VSOE Pullman set in tow for a special running to Northfleet in Kent on 6 September 1985, Class 73/1 electro-diesel No 73112 passes Charlton station, in southeast London.
Brian Morrison

THREE

THE FREIGHT SCENE

During the past few years British Rail's freight business has undergone a quiet revolution, both in operational and management techniques. Traditional, but unremunerative, vacuum-braked or partially fitted mixed loads linking labour-intensive marshalling yards are nearly a thing of the past, although the virtual demise of this type of operation has not necessarily resulted in the business being lost to road transport, as a considerable amount has gone over to the Railfreight Sector's fast-growing Speedlink services which are also attracting many new customers.

Coal and coke merry-go-round trains make up almost half of BR's freight income, with the remainder resulting from significant contributions from the movement of aggregates, cement, steel, oil, grain, chemicals, bricks, motor vehicles and refuse etc. In addition, van traffic caters for the carriage of newspapers, parcels and some remaining perishables and, of course, there is also the vital role of both Freightliner Ltd and the block workings involving privately-owned wagons.

Locomotive power ranges from the 204bhp of the Class 03s to the 3,300bhp of the Class 58s, with almost every current class of BR locomotive being utilised in some way or another.

Below:
Crewe-built Class 56 Co-Co No 56131 passes Low Fell on 20 June 1985 hauling loaded Merry-go-round hoppers from Swalwell Colliery to Tyne yard for distribution.
Peter J. Robinson

Above:

A brace of InterCity-liveried Class 87/0 electric locomotives, with No 87003 *Patriot* leading No 87006 *City of Glasgow* on a Willesden-Glasgow Gushetfaulds Freightliner service, pictured in the Lune Valley on 28 June 1986. Note the differing forms of this livery carried by the two locomotives. *Peter J. Robinson*

Below:

The Class 58 Co-Co fleet of locomotives represent dedicated power for Railfreight's most important traffic. On 18 February 1985 No 58024 hauls an up coal-laden MGR train along the Erewash Valley line at Bennerley, Ilkeston. The disused viaduct in the background once carried Great Northern Railway tracks to Derby Friargate. *Colin J. Marsden*

Bottom:

It isn't often that a Class 31 A1A-A1A is given charge of a rake of MGR wagons, or that such a train should have a brakevan! All is not as it seems, however, as No 31139 comes off the former Midland Railway line through Castle Donnington and joins the main Derby-Burton/Crewe route at Stenson Junction on 1 July 1983; the train is heading northwards for the hoppers to be serviced. *Brian Morrison*

Top:
With a long haul of ARC hoppers, Class 56 No 56047 is held in a Westbury siding on the evening of 31 August 1984 and will proceed westwards on the following morning.
Brian Morrison

Above:
A locomotive class other than 47, 37, 31 or 08 at Ripple Lane yards, Barking, is somewhat unusual and for a Class 33 to be in attendance on oil tanks is extremely rare. On 23 September 1985, No 33038 heads back to Furzebrook oil terminal and more familiar Southern Region metals.
Brian Morrison

Left:
A Class 37 cautiously winds its load of chemical tanks across the pointwork at the north of Newcastle station on 29 May 1980. *Brian Morrison*

Below:
Class 20 Bo-Bo locomotives Nos 20077 and 20141 round the curve at Buxworth with empty 'Peakstone' hoppers from Northwich, returning to one of the Peak District quarries on 30 May 1985. *Ian Gould*

Right:
On 3 April 1985, Class 56 No 56075 heads south at Besborough, between Market Harborough and Kettering, with a Tarmac stone train. *Bill Sharman*

Below right:
Class 56 locomotives Nos 56039 and 56088 leave Llanwern on 19 May 1986 with a train of empty hoppers for Port Talbot. *Mike Jones*

Fly-ash wagons from Ratcliffe-on-Soar power station to the CEGB Fletton tip pass Sutton Bonington, on the Midland main line, on 27 June 1983 with motive power provided by Class 56 No 56098. Why someone has felt obliged to scrawl the last three digits of the TOPS number in very amateurish fashion below the air-horn covers is not known. *Brian Morrison*

Below left:

Disparate liveried Class 73/1 electro-diesels Nos 73132 and 73141 work in multiple on 19 April 1985 at Tolworth, Surrey, with a Hall Aggregates train from Newhaven stone terminal. *Colin J. Marsden*

Below:

The attractive livery applied to Class 73/1 No 73102 *Air Tour Suisse* for the 'Gatwick Express' services looks a little incongruous when the locomotive is rostered for a freight turn. On 13 July 1985 a rake of Rugby Cement wagons at St Denys, near Southampton, heads for Halling cement works in Kent via Hoo Junction, having emanated from Bevois Park. *John Vaughan*

Right:

The four General Motors locomotives constructed in the USA for Foster Yeoman commenced working a number of stone trains from Merehead Quarry in February 1986. Owned and operated exclusively by Foster Yeoman, they are the first private-owner locomotives to be allowed to work on BR main lines; albeit with BR drivers. Incorporating transport of stone with driver training, No 59002 *Yeoman Enterprise* is seen on the Purfleet-Merehead empties at Ealing Broadway on 15 August 1986. *John E. Oxley*

Above :
**Class 20 No 20163, in Railfreight livery, heads a permanent way
train at Nuneaton on 7 May 1986.** *Chris Milner*

Above:
Nicely lined-out 'Peak' Class 45/0 No 45013 passes Dudley signalbox, on the freight-only line from Stourbridge Junction to Pleck Junction, Walsall, with an ABS freight for Bescot on 3 June 1985. *Brian J. Robbins*

Below:
On 1 July 1985 an ABS from Scunthorpe to Craiginches Yard, Aberdeen, consists primarily of Grainflow Polybulks and steel-carrying wagons as Class 37 No 37006 takes the load through Stone Bridge, Durham. Note the two headlights fitted to the locomotive in place of the usual boxed marker lights. *Peter J. Robinson*

Below:
A St Blazey-Goonbarrow ABS composed of two English China Clay bogie hoppers leased from Tiger Rail Ltd and two Cargowaggons heads down the Newquay branch at Luxulyan on 3 October powered by Cornish Railways Class 37 No 37207 *William Cookworthy*. *Brian Morrison*

Below right:
An early morning haul of clay hoods from Moorswater Dries for unloading at Carne Point, runs along the freight only section of line from Moorswater to Coombe Junction on 2 October 1985 hauled by Class 37 No 37247. The 1,750bhp

'Siphons' are permitted to haul 22 loaded clay hoods up the gradient to Liskeard and this view appears to be of a maximum loading. *Brian Morrison*

Bottom:
Class 37s No 37222 and Cornish Railways No 37196 *Tre Pol and Pen*, known locally as 'the twins', shunt china clay hoods at Parkandillack Dries on the same day. These wagons are now used only on local trip workings, to and from the various dries and Carne Point, with the PBA 'Tigers' taking over for the ABS services to the Potteries.
Brian Morrison

Right:
Class 47/0 No 47098, of Crewe diesel depot, passes West Ealing on 3 August 1985 hauling the Saturday Ripple Lane-Southampton Maritime Freightliner. *John Vaughan*

Below right:
A long haul of covered 'Cartics' bypass Crewe on the 'independent lines' on 3 July 1985 headed by Class 85 Bo-Bo electric No 85005. The train is the Ford Motor Co 12.27 Garston-Dagenham Dock. *John Vaughan*

Below:
With the last snow of the winter proving reluctant to disappear, Class 37 No 37092 snarls up Belstead Bank, near Ipswich, on 16 February 1985 with a heavy ABS freight that includes open 'Cartics' for Mossend from Parkeston Quay. *Michael J. Collins*

Above:
A Tinsley-allocated Class 37, No 37125, heads a Sheffield-London parcels train between the tunnels at Welwyn, Hertfordshire, on 19 August 1978.
Antony Guppy

Right:
Class 73/1 electro-diesel No 73120 runs between New Malden and Raynes Park on 6 March 1985 hauling the 08.45 empty vans from Eastleigh to Clapham Junction yard.
Colin J. Marsden

Above:
A haul of steel coil from British Steel, Lackenby to British Steel, Corby passes Clay Cross, Derbyshire, on 6 March 1985 powered by snowplough-fitted Class 37 No 37096 working in multiple with sister locomotive No 37042. Both locomotives are a part of the Thornaby allocation.
Bert Wynn

Below:
Looking very smart in newly applied Railfreight Sector grey paint, Class 31/1 No 31160 backs its freight train into a siding at Eastfield signalbox, Peterborough, having arrived from the south on 7 March 1986.   *Bill Sharman*

Right:
At many sidings can be found brake vans of various types gently rotting away; the advent of air-braked services and the demise of unfitted and partially-fitted mixed freights having led to their virtual disappearance from use on BR. On 3 April 1980, No 40143 hauls a train of empty mineral wagons on a Sandhills-Penmaenmawr working past Olive Mount.   *J. S. Buckley*

Below right:
Class 31/1 No 31139 leaves Newcastle with a down train of empty wagons on 29 May 1980.   *Brian Morrison*

Above:
**The 10.36 driver-training
special from Hither Green to
the Kent Coast approaches
Swanley, Kent, on
6 September 1985.
Class 415/2 4-EPB EMUs
Nos 5355 and 5310 are being
hauled by Class 56
No 56047.** *Brian Morrison*

Right:
**Having completed the re-
railment of a recalcitrant
Class 415/1 EMU that formed
the 09.02 Dartford-Charing
Cross via Eltham train, the
Hither Green breakdown
train, including Rapier
steam crane
No ADRR95209, prepares to
return home from Dartford
on 8 January 1985 hauled by
BRC&W Class 33/0
No 33047.** *Brian Morrison*

FOUR

ON DEPOT

In the steam days of the 1950s there were some 332 engine sheds with a locomotive allocation, and very many more if the various sub-sheds were included. Today just 90 depots have a motive power allocation with another 31 listed as stabling or fuelling points. Many famous names from the past still exist, such as Old Oak Common, Bristol Bath Road, Willesden, Crewe, Carlisle, Newton Heath, Stratford, Norwich, York, Gateshead, Inverness, Eastfield, Stewarts Lane and Eastleigh. Many more, however, are merely names from an old Ian Allan *abc*. Camden, Rugby, New England, 'Top Link' King's Cross, Kittybrewster, St Margarets, Nine Elms and Exmouth Junction have all gone.

The smells are different today, the buildings are, for the most part, of modern and functional design and maintenance techniques are advanced to the extent that diesel and electric traction leaves far less work residue. One thing that remains, however, is the indefinable atmosphere. Whether it is a steam shed or a maintenance depot, that at least is still with us.

Below:
On 8 May 1984, Class 87/0 Bo-Bo electric locomotive No 87012 *Coeur de Lion* **peers out of Willesden Depot awaiting a media audience before officially unveiling the new InterCity 'Executive' livery in which it had been repainted.** *Brian Morrison*

The colourful scene at Glasgow Eastfield on 12 June 1985. Apart from the standard liveried locomotives of Classes 08, 27 and 37, the visual highpoint consists of the Class 37 'Highland Terriers' Nos 37043 *Loch Lomond*, 37081 *Loch Long* and 37191 *International Youth Year 1985*.   *Tom Noble*

Left:
Class 31/4 A1A-A1A No 31404, with white body stripe, stands in Bounds Green depot on 26 July 1979 with a train of Mk 1 stock which is being cleaned prior to use.
Brian Morrison

Right:
With closure imminent, Westhouses depot has clearly seen better days as Class 20 No 20163 pauses between duties on the Erewash Valley freights on a dull 29 June 1983.
Brian Morrison

Above:

A colourful line-up inside Old Oak Common depot for the 1985 Open Day with restored Class 35 'Hymek' No D7018 in original green livery, preserved Class 52 'Western' No D1015 *Western Champion* in golden ochre livery, together with Class 50 No 50007 *Sir Edward Elgar* and Class 47/4 No 47500 *Great Western* both in GWR green as a part of the GWR150 activities. *Colin J. Marsden*

Left:

Re-fuelling completed, Class 33/1 No 33103 waits to take the short journey from Stewarts Lane depot to Waterloo station on 12 October 1985 in order to power the 14.10 Waterloo-Salisbury train *Brian Morrison*

Above right:

At Cardiff Canton's Open Day on 6 July 1985, two of the special exhibits were Class 58 Co-Co No 58003 and Derby RTC Bo-Bo No 97201 *Experiment* (ex-Class 24 No 24061). *Colin J. Marsden*

Right:

Class 37 No 37104 receives attention inside Thornaby depot on 18 May 1982 alongside a Class 08 shunter and a Class 47. *Stephen Montgomery*

Above:
**In sub-zero conditions it is
common practice to keep
engines ticking over in
order to avoid any freeze-up.
This is the case in this view
at Bescot depot, including
Class 45/0s Nos 45046,
45005 and 45069, with
Class 56 No 56090 at the
rear.** *Malcolm Inger*

Right:
**If one really tries, trains can
be found in peculiar places!
On 18 June 1984 Class 415/2
4-EPB EMU No 5364 is
actually stabled in a siding
at Blackfriars station
awaiting the next turn of
duty as part of the evening
commuter services.**
Brian Morrison

FIVE

TODAY'S MOTIVE POWER – OLD AND NEW

Of the locomotive class numbers allocated for the purposes of TOPS, ranging originally from 01 to 55, only 15 main types remain in service today plus three new varieties, Classes 56, 58 and 59. This rather bald statement, however, does not take into account the large number of variants within some of the types — and the consequent sub-classes created — and the interest in locomotives remains as high as ever. The majority of the representative classes of DMU, DEMU and EMU are also featured in this section with due emphasis being given to the older types being phased out and the newcomers that are making those older types look even older!

Below:
The Class 305 EMU fleet was constructed from 1960 for use on the Liverpool Street suburban services. The blue and grey livery now applied has improved their appearance and some now sport a 'Jazz Train' motif between the cab windows as with this example, No 305408, passing Stratford on 3 September 1984 coupled to 305417 with ecs for Liverpool Street. *Brian Morrison*

Bottom:
The Class 307s were introduced in 1956 for use on the Great Eastern outer-suburban lines. All are 4-car sets allocated to Ilford. On 3 September 1984 No 307128 heads away from Stratford yards and makes for Liverpool Street with ecs to form a train for Shenfield. *Brian Morrison*

Above:

On the same day, Class 309/2 express EMU No 309616 uses the up fast line at Stratford and leads unit No 309612 on a Clacton-Liverpool Street train. These types were introduced in 1961 and built at BR York expressly for the Clacton and Walton services, on which they still operate with distinction up to the present time. *Brian Morrison*

Below:

The first batch of new generation EMU stock emerged from BREL York in 1976 for use on the Great Northern inner-suburban area. These 64 3-car sets, designated Class 313, were followed in 1979 by a further batch of 16 high density units for the Glasgow Suburban lines classified 314. Unit No 314213 is seen at Partick on 31 May 1983 forming a Glasgow Central-Milngavie service and lettered 'Trans-Clyde'. *Les Nixon*

Above:
**Apart from the distinctive 'Strathclyde Transport' livery
and the pantograph, the new Class 318 EMUs constructed at
BREL Derby and York could be mistaken for a Southern
Region Class 455/9. Twenty-one of these units came into use
on Ayrshire line services in September 1986 and the first of
them, No 318250, was previewed for the media on 6 June
1986 and is pictured here at Glasgow Central after working
as a special to and from Lanark.** *Stuart Marshall*

Above right:
**The Class 411 4-CEP 'Kent Coasters' have been the basic
power for the Kent Coast electrified system for more than
30 years, having been constructed at Eastleigh Works from
1955. The complete fleet was given extensive refurbishment
at Swindon Works between 1976 and 1984 to include
aluminium framed tinted glass windows, new design seats,
lowered ceilings and fluorescent lighting. On 6 September
1985, unit No 1579 leads a Class 423 4-VEP No 7892 at
Gillingham, Kent, forming the 11.52 train from London
Victoria to Dover Priory via Herne Hill and Canterbury
East.** *Brian Morrison*

Right:
**The first of the 213 Class 415 4-EPB EMUs emerged from
Eastleigh in 1951; a more modern version of the Southern
Railway's 4-SUB fleet with electro-pneumatic brakes and
buck-eye couplings. During the period 1974-84 just under a
quarter of them were 'facelifted' and re-classified as 415/4.
On 14 August 1985, Class 415/1 No 5123 leaves Waterloo East
making up the rear of the 15.08 Charing Cross-Orpington
local service whilst Class 415/4 No 5461 arrives as the 14.20
Reigate-Charing Cross.** *Brian Morrison*

The approaches to Waterloo in May 1984 with, from left to right, Class 491 4-car trailer control unit No 429 leading a Bournemouth semi-fast, Class 421/2 4-CIG No 7344 at the head of a fast service for Portsmouth Harbour and Class 423 4-VEP No 7747 at the rear of an arrival. The 28 Class 491 4-TCs were constructed at York from 1966 for use with the 4-REP units on the electrified Bournemouth line. The 138 4-CIGs were built at York in three batches from 1964 to 1970 and were utilised on the Brighton, Portsmouth and Guildford/Reading services and replaced the old 4-COR series. All 194 of the 4-car high density 4-VEPs were also built at York from 1967 and operate throughout the Southern Region electrified system. *Brian Morrison*

The Class 420 4-BIGs were first introduced in 1965 when 18 4-car buffet units were built at York for use with the 4-CIGs on the Victoria-Brighton and South Coast lines with a further batch of 10 following in 1970 for the Waterloo-Portsmouth services. Now classified as 422/1, No 2101 passes Streatham North Junction on 30 May 1985 leading the 11.50 Victoria-Ore and is passed in the opposite direction by the 10.30 Hastings-Victoria with a Class 421/2 No 7399 bringing up the rear. *Colin J. Marsden*

Left:

Constructed at Eastleigh in 1957/58 for the Euston-Watford and Broad Street-Richmond services, the 57 three-car Class 501 EMUs have now been phased out and replaced by Southern Region Class 416/3 2-EPBs. During their last days, on 18 September 1985, No 501142 arrives at Euston from Watford Junction. *Brian J. Robbins*

Below left:

Motive power for the Isle of Wight system is provided by former London Transport underground stock, which even retains the clerestory roofs of the period in which it was manufactured — the late 1920s! As the island loading gauge is smaller than that on the mainland, this stock was purchased from London Transport rather than go to the expense of heightening most of the system's bridges in order to run modern standard stock. Before the stock was painted blue and white, the Ryde Pier Head-Ryde Esplanade shuttle crosses the pier over the Solent headed by Class 486 3-TIS unit No 031. *M. Pope*

Below:

The Southern Region's new generation 4-car EMU, the Class 455, began to appear from BREL York in 1982, mainly for use on the suburban network radiating from Waterloo. They replaced the Class 508s which had been used on the Southern Region as an interim measure prior to being transferred to Merseyside to replace the life-expired Class 503s. On 10 June 1986, Class 455/9 No 5908 waits to leave Waterloo with a Dorking service whilst Network SouthEast liveried Class 455/8 No 5872 forms a special in connection with the Sector's media launch of that day. Note the much cleaner front end arrangement of the newer unit. *Brian Morrison*

Right:
**Three of the four cars that made up Class 508 EMU
No 508016 now operate on Merseyside as unit No 508116.
During their sojourn on Southern Region metals, the 09.05
from Chessington South arrives at Waterloo station on
22 October 1983.** *R. S. Freeman*

Below right:
**The most modern of the Southern Region's fleet of DEMUs
are the 19 3-car sets that make up Class 207 introduced from
Eastleigh in 1962 for use on the SR's non-electrified lines
but, specifically, on the Oxted services. On 10 August 1985,
No 1304 passes the unusual split distant signal near
Birchden Junction whilst working the 09.24 Victoria-
Uckfield service. The signal was removed following closure
of the Tunbridge Wells-Groombridge line.** *John Vaughan*

Below:
**In 1981 two prototype DEMUs, one 3-car and the other 4-car,
emerged from Derby Works for evaluation and were
classified as Class 210. Allocated to Reading depot and
working regularly on the Paddington suburban services
they have proved popular, but further construction is
unlikely on the grounds of cost. On 1 November 1984 the
3-car unit No 210002 waits to depart from Paddington as
the 15.04 to Reading.** *Colin J. Marsden*

Far right:
**By far the largest fleet of DMUs operating on BR metals are
the Metropolitan-Cammell Class 101 sets with over 600 cars
of the same basic design being constructed over a four year
period from 1956. They can be coupled into 2-, 3- or 4-car
formations and, here, a 2-car London Midland Region set
passes Marsh Brook in the Border Counties, on the old
'North & West' Route, forming the 15.50 Shrewsbury-
Swansea service. The train will take to the Central Wales
line at Craven Arms.** *John Vaughan*

Above left:
Passengers board BR Derby Class 108 driving trailer composite No M54269 at Manchester Victoria on 30 May 1984. This substantial fleet of low density units numbers over 300 and can be coupled into 2-, 3- or 4-car formations. All are allocated to Eastern and London Midland Regions. *Brian Morrison*

Above:
On 21 August 1984, a 2-car Birmingham RC&W DMU of Class 110 departs eastwards from Lincoln Central and passes over Pelham Street Crossing, forming the 14.37 to Boston. These Rolls-Royce-engined 'Calder Valley' units date from 1961 and all are allocated to the Eastern Region. *Bill Sharman*

Left:
Another of the larger DMU classes when constructed from 1956-59 was the Cravens Class 105, with nearly 250 cars in service. Drastic inroads into them have been made, however, and it will not be long before a scene such as this at Newcastle on 29 May 1980 will be something from the past. A 2-car Class 105 leads here with a local train for Alnmouth. *Brian Morrison*

Above right:
An interesting development of recent years is the prototype Class 140 DMU developed at Derby Works from the LEV railbus and constructed from Leyland National bus body components, mounted on a railway underframe. On 18 April 1985 the unit appeared unexpectedly with a Plymouth-Par driver training special and is seen passing Tywardreath near Par in Cornwall. *John Vaughan*

Right:
Another type of DMU which closely follows the standard design are the 15 3-car units that make up the Birmingham RC&W Class 118. Introduced in 1959 for Western Region suburban use, all are allocated to Plymouth Laira or Bristol Bath Road, On 17 April 1985 a unit reduced to a twin set passes Luxulyan forming the 17.43 Par-Newquay service, made up of DMS No W51320 and DMBS No W51305. *John Vaughan*

Top right:

Built for BR by Gloucester RC&W in 1958, the 25 Cross-country sets that make up Class 119 all have the familiar 'Derby' front end appearance. Due to line closures, members of the class have been quite extensively moved about the country and all have had their original buffets taken out of use. A present-day role for the Reading-based units is upon the Reading-Tonbridge and Reading-Gatwick Airport trains where the buffet area has been replaced by passenger luggage space. On an autumnal 15 November 1984, unit No L579 traverses Southern Region metals beneath the North Downs, near Dorking, and forms the 12.12 Gatwick Airport-Reading service.
John Vaughan

Right:

The Class 120 Cross-country 3-car DMUs were constructed at Swindon Works between 1957 and 1960. Like the Class 119s they have been switched about from area to area as a result of line closures, and the original buffet areas are now removed. On 27 June 1983, a 3-car unit running with a Metro-Cammell centre trailer forms a Matlock-Derby train approaching Duffield.
Brian Morrison

Bottom right:

The fleet of 15 single power cars and eight driving trailer seconds that makes up the 23 coaches of the Pressed Steel Co-built Class 121 were constructed in 1960 for branch line and local services and, in many ways, were the BR equivalent of the original GWR Railcars. For the GWR150 celebrations in 1985, certain locomotives and stock were painted in the GWR livery of chocolate and cream. One of the examples was Class 121 DMBS No W55020 which, on 20 July 1985, formed the 16.05 Ealing Broadway-Greenford local service.
John Vaughan

The Gloucester RC&W single parcels vans are known as DMLVs and are classified as Class 128. All are provided with a driving position at each end and three sets of double doors along the bodyside for mail and goods, and they have two Leyland Albion 6-cylinder engines of 230bhp. One such car, No W55991, scuttles down the Western main line near Twyford on 21 June 1984 forming the 15.55 Paddington-Reading parcels service. *Brian Morrison*

Left:

A derivative of the prototype Class 140 is the wide-bodied Leyland National/BR Derby Class 142 DMU which entered service on BR during late 1985. No 142008 passes Colleyhurst, Miles Platting, on 9 November 1985 smartly attired in the attractive livery of the Greater Manchester PTE.
Hugh Ballantyne

Below left:

Two Class 150 3-car prototype DMUs were constructed at BREL York Works in 1984, one powered by 285bhp Cummins engines and the second with 280bhp Rolls-Royce 'Eagles'. On 24 May 1985 the Rolls-Royce-powered unit No 150002 is pictured at Matlock after working the 14.20 train from Derby. *Stuart Marshall*

Right:

The Class 253 and 254 InterCity 125 trains were introduced from 1976 and 1977 respectively. The 253s consist of a rake of seven or eight Mk 3 coaches with a power car at each end, whilst the 254s include eight or nine cars to allow for the slightly higher loadings required on the East Coast main line services. With the changeover from the original blue and grey livery to the red and grey of the InterCity Sector, mixed formations with power cars and trailers in different combinations of colours were a common sight. On 11 January 1986, the 07.00 Plymouth-Newcastle train passes Church Road, south of Birmingham. *A. Swift*

Below:

Ordered at the same time as the prototype Class 150 units were the futuristic-looking Metropolitan-Cammell Class 151 prototypes which arrived at Derby in 1985 for evaluation. On 17 April 1985 two cars of 3-car unit No 151001 climb the Lickey Bank on test from Bromsgrove. *Brian J. Robbins*

Above:

The mammoth fleet of Class 08 diesel shunters once totalled 1,193 examples and many are still in service today — a tribute to the success of the design. Having been repainted in green at Tyseley, and carrying smart name and numberplates, No 08604 *Phantom* is seen at Birmingham New Street on 20 June 1986. *Chris Morrison*

Below:

The fleet of Class 20 Bo-Bo locomotives was introduced from 1957, built at the English Electric Vulcan Foundry. They are usually found coupled in pairs working on a variety of freight trains on Eastern, London Midland and Scottish Regions but are still used on passenger turns as the occasion demands. Also popular for railtours, Nos 20184 and 20169 are so employed rounding the sea wall approaching Teignmouth on 8 July 1984 with a special . *Brian Morrison*

Above:
The large fleet of Type 2 Bo-Bo Class 25 locomotives was introduced in 1961 as uprated versions of the Class 24s which entered service from 1957. They were constructed at the BR works of Crewe, Darlington and Derby and also at the Gorton Works of Beyer Peacock Ltd. Large numbers have been withdrawn during the past few years and their total demise is imminent. On 4 July 1985, Class 25/2 No 25200 passes Bayston Hill, in the delightful border country of Shrewsbury, with a load of ballast for Guide Bridge, the locomotive having run round its train at Dorrington. *John Vaughan*

Below:
Rather akin to the Class 24/25 relationship, the Class 27s are uprated and improved versions of the earlier Class 26s, which were the first main line diesel electric locomotives to be constructed at the Smethwick works of Birmingham RC&W from 1958, with the 1,250bhp Class 27 being introduced from 1960. Both types have spent most of their lives in Scotland. On 5 June 1982 No 27018 leaves Markinch with the 09.21 Edinburgh-Dundee service. *B. Galloway*

Above:
The Class 31 A1A-A1A fleet of Type 2 locomotives was introduced during the days of steam in 1957 and constructed at the Loughborough Works of Brush Electrical Machines Ltd. Earlier teething troubles overcome, the locomotives are now a success story and can be seen on all four English Regions hauling a variety of both passenger and freight traffic. Passing Clay Cross Junction on 26 June 1985, No 31309 hauls a down freight off the Erewash Valley line. *Les Nixon*

Right:
To satisfy the Southern Region's requirements for a main line locomotive fleet in the Type 3 category, an order for 98 was given to the BRC&W Co for construction at their Smethwick Works and the first emerged in 1959. The same basic body shell as that used on the Class 26s was utilised with a number of detail differences. The power unit, however, was an excellent 1,550bhp Sulzer. This pair of 'Cromptons' was photographed at Basingstoke on 29 September 1984. On the left is Class 33/1 'push-pull' variant No 33111 with the 14.10 Waterloo-Salisbury, while on the right is Class 33/0 No 33012 with the diverted Cardiff Central-Portsmouth Harbour service. *John Vaughan*

Below right:
The 230 locomotives of Class 37 were constructed between 1960 and 1965 by both the English Electric Co at Newton-le-Willows and by the Robert Stephenson & Hawthorn Works at Darlington. Powered by an English Electric 12CSVT engine producing up to 1,750bhp these Type 3 Co-Co locomotives can literally be seen from Caithness to Cornwall, where they operate with equal success. No 37165 leaves Standedge Tunnel at Diggle on 26 March 1982 with a westbound haul of tanks. *Bill Chapman*

Above:
Surely the most famous locomotive running on BR during the mid-1980s must be green-liveried Class 40 No 40122/D200, retained for use on special services such as this Scottish Railway Preservation Society charter to Kyle of Lochalsh, seen at Gleneagles on 28 June 1986. *Bert Wynn*

Right:
During 1985 a number of withdrawn Class 40 1Co-Co1 locomotives were resuscitated from the scrap lines for use as departmental locomotives during the big Crewe re-signalling operation. Standing at the head of an overhead catenary special working on 3 July 1985 is the former No 40118, renumbered 97408.
John Vaughan

60

Above:
Passing through delightful countryside at Respryn Bridge, between Lostwithiel and Bodmin Parkway stations, on 18 April 1985 is 'Peak' Class 45/0 No 45069 hauling the 09.38 ABS freight from St Blazey to Severn Tunnel Junction. The original 10 Sulzer-engined 2,300bhp 'Peaks', designated Class 44, were withdrawn from service in 1980. The main batch of this Type 4 1Co-Co1 design, had an uprated 2,500bhp Sulzer engine and was divided into three types: the steam heat boilered 45/0s, those fitted for electric train heating and classified 45/1, and the batch fitted with Brush electrical equipment and given TOPS classification 46. Overall the 'Peaks' have given outstanding service to BR for over a quarter of a century. *John Vaughan*

Below:
The Brush Group's Falcon Works at Loughborough produced the first of the Class 47s in September 1962. By early 1967, no fewer than 512 locomotives of the class had been built at Loughborough and at BR Crewe and the excellent Type 4 had become the largest class of main line diesel-electric locomotive in the country. In the last week of operation of Ely South signalbox, Class 47/4 No 47506 blasts away from Ely past the many semaphore signals that have now been removed, hauling the 17.30 for Liverpool Street on 20 June 1985. *John Vaughan*

Left:
Fifty Class 50s were built by English Electric at their Vulcan Foundry Works at Newton-le-Willows in 1967-68 for use on the northern sections of the West Coast main line that had still to be electrified. Fitted for multiple-unit working by Crewe Works in 1969, the 2,700bhp machines succesfully worked in pairs with heavy trains over the severely graded route, including Shap and Beattock Banks, until the fully electrified Euston-Glasgow service started in May 1975. Prior to this, some of the class had been undergoing trials on Western Region and, eventually, all were transferrred to Old Oak Common, Bristol and Laira, allowing the WR to withdraw the much-loved but non-standard Class 52 'Western' fleet. Advent of the HSTs resulted in the class being found work on the Waterloo-Exeter services and on many of the inter-regional expresses to and from the West Country. On 3 July 1984, No 50010 *Monarch* forges through the Devon countryside at Worth, near Exeter, with the 10.27 Paddington-Penzance express which consists of all first class stock. *Brian Morrison*

Left:

A significant increase in the movement of coal by rail required a Type 5 freight locomotive capable of heavy, long-distance haulage. The success of the Class 47s ensured that Brush obtained the contract for the first 30 machines, which were built at the Brush Group's Romanian counterpart of Electroputere which commenced delivery in 1976. BREL Doncaster took up the building from No 56031 and the total fleet of 135 locomotives was completed at Crewe to allow Doncaster to make a start on the Class 58s. On 16 June 1984 No 56031 *Merehead* is seen near the village of Great Bedwyn, on the Berks & Hants line, hauling Yeoman Procor stone hoppers towards Westbury.
John Vaughan

Above:

Constructed by General Motors of the USA, four Co-Co diesel-electric locomotives powered by GM 16-cylinder engines of the same 3,300bhp output as the Class 58s, were delivered to these shores in 1985 to the order of Foster Yeoman for exclusive use on their stone trains to and from Merehead Quarry, near Frome. Being allowed to operate over BR metals, they have been designated TOPS Class 59. Prior to being named *Yeoman Challenger*, No 59004 departs from Acton Yard with stone for Northfleet terminal.
Jean Marsden

Below left:

Despite the success of the Class 56s they were an expensive locomotive to construct. Present-day finances and technology brought about Class 58. This Type 5 locomotive is of a completely new design, being assembled from 'pre-made' component parts bolted on to a rigid frame. Power is provided by a 12-cylinder GEC-Ruston engine capable of 3,300bhp. Fifty of the type have been constructed at BREL Doncaster, with the first delivered in November 1982. On 19 June 1985, No 58015 works into Westhouses with empty HAA Merry-go-round hoppers.   *John Vaughan*

Below:

The 09.48 Southampton-Halling 'Rugby Cement' train passes Farnborough on 6 August 1983 headed by Class 73/0 electro-diesel No 73003. Capable of operating from the Southern Region third rail or being able to obtain traction from their own diesel engine/generator set, the class of 49 locomotives was constructed from 1962 at Eastleigh Works and from 1965 at English Electric's Vulcan Foundry. The electro-diesel concept was a very clever one and it is perhaps surprising that the principle has not been furthered on other regions of BR.   *R. T. Nunn*

On 17 August 1984, Class 81 electric locomotive No 81019 prepares to depart from Euston with a summer special of Mk 1 stock whilst, in the background, Class 87/0 No 87032 *Kenilworth* awaits departure time with the 15.50 for Manchester Piccadilly. The Class 81s were the first of the West Coast main line's new fleet of locomotives, having been ordered from Associated Electrical Industries who, in turn, sub-contracted the actual locomotive construction to Birmingham RC&W; they were introduced for driver and staff training from November 1959. The Class 82s appeared in May 1960 from AEI/Metrovick with building undertaken by Beyer Peacock; the Class 83s came from English Electric; the Class 84s from the North British Locomotive Co of Glasgow; and the Class 85s from AEI/GEC with the construction taking place at BR Doncaster. *Brian Morrison*

Above:
Having gained considerable experience in the operation of electric locomotives, British Rail set about the introduction of a second generation of 100 machines, the Class 86s. Equipment for these was supplied by AEI/English Electric, mechanical construction being undertaken by BR Doncaster and English Electric. The Class 87s appeared in 1973 from BREL Crewe, with equipment supplied by GEC Traction Ltd, and with GEC traction motors generating 5,000bhp compared to the 3,600bhp from the AEI equipment in the Class 86s. The differing front end appearance of the two types is obvious from this scene at Euston with Class 86/2 No 86220 *Goliath* on the left and No 87012 *Coeur de Lion* on the right waiting to depart with expresses for Liverpool Lime Street and Carlisle.
Brian Morrison

BR LIVERIES FOR THE 1980s

There is no doubt that British Rail is rapidly losing its old 'corporate image' as local colour schemes take over both motive power and stock from one end of the system to the other. From Highland Rail and ScotRail, from the InterCity, Railfreight, Network SouthEast and Provincial Sectors and from the likes of the PTEs of Strathclyde, West Yorkshire, Greater Manchester and West Midlands comes a variety of colour that is supplemented by odd variants of GWR brown and cream, GWR lined green, British Telecom yellow, Red Star red and the strange looking maroon and white apparition sponsored by a local tourist authority with regard to a West Highland shuttle! Some of the liveries are elegant, some are attractive but not very functional, and others are downright weird. More are yet to come no doubt as the fashion takes hold. At least it provides a field-day for the colour photographer.

Below:
With power car No 43125 *Merchant Venturer* bringing up the rear of the train, the 07.45 Paddington-Penzance crosses Tregeagle Viaduct, between St Austell and Truro, on 24 August 1985 beautifully turned out in complete InterCity livery. *John Vaughan*

Top:
Highland Rail livery, with the large Scottish terrier emblem relative to the size of the bodyside number and BR logo, adorns the flanks of Class 37 No 37188 *Jimmy Shand* hauling a weed-killing train down the Oban line on 31 May 1985 and passing Tyndrum Lower.   *Dorothy Robinson*

Above:
On 17 August 1985 new-look Scottish Class 26 No 26026 in Railfreight livery brightens up the environs of Perth.
Tom Noble

Top right:
Class 37/4 No 37426 *Bont-y-Bermo* heads the 10-coach formation of InterCity-liveried Mk 1 stock making up the 07.25 summer Saturdays only Birmingham-Aberystwyth train at Ynyslas on 9 August 1986.   *Geoffrey Bannister*

Right:
In a breathtaking setting at Golant on the River Fowey, Class 37 No 37196 *Tre Pol and Pen*, in attractive Railfreight livery, works in multiple with No 37222 heading down the Fowey Branch with loaded china clay hoods on the brilliantly clear evening of 3 October 1985.   *Brian Morrison*

Above:
The first locomotive to appear in the Railfreight Sector's distinctive livery was Class 58 No 58001, seen here passing along the Crewe Independent Lines during the period that Crewe station was closed for major resignalling and relaying of trackwork. The train is a Garston-Toton coal empties and was photographed on 3 July 1985.
John Vaughan

Below:
The large fleet of Class 47s seems destined to appear in a variety of liveries, from the Stratford-applied silver roof and black window surrounds, through ScotRail, InterCity, GWR Green, Network SouthEast, Railfreight and large logo and number types to just plain blue. Sporting the colours of the Railfreight Sector, No 47050 hauls a train of tanks from Immingham to Sheffield Tinsley on 22 August 1985 and passes Mexborough. Michael J. Collins

Introduced in 1957 in, what was then, BR green with a silver roof and subsequently given the corporate treatment of 'Rail blue', few people may have expected the Class 20 fleet to appear in Railfreight grey but, in fact, they are being so treated — and very flattering it looks too on No 20023 seen at Tyseley, Birmingham, on 27 April 1985. *T. R. Dungate*

Another type to justify the new Railfreight image is the Class 31/1. On 5 September 1985 No 31158 approaches Shaldon Bridge, Teignmouth, hauling an up parcels train. *Stephen Montgomery*

InterCity
47 406
Rail Riders

Left:

The first Class 47 to receive InterCity paintwork was No 47406 *Railriders* seen here near Durham on 4 November 1985 hauling the 09.23 Newcastle-Penzance train. It will be pleasant when all the stock can match the locomotives. *Peter J. Robinson*

Below:

InterCity Sector livery looks particularly smart when it is kept clean and when the coaching stock matches. With a Mk 3 sleeping car coupled next to the locomotive, Class 87/0 No 87016 *Sir Francis Drake* is pictured at Euston with the 17.03 service for Holyhead on 13 August 1986. *John E. Oxley*

Bottom:

When put into BR's plain blue livery the Class 73 electro-diesel fleet looked particularly mundane and rather akin to the oft-described 'box on wheels'. Some now sport the livery of the InterCity Sector for operating the 'Gatwick Express' diagrams, whilst others, including the first member of the class, No 73001, have received the attractive grey roof, black window surrounds and large BR logo and TOPS number treatment. On 30 May 1986, the Class 73/0 waits to depart Clapham yard with empty coaching stock. *Brian Morrison*

Below:
During the months of resignalling the Brighton main line, certain Inter-Regional trains started their journey from Hove, on the West Coastway line. On 7 May 1985 there was an interloper of note. Sporting its large Scottish terrier motif is No 47593 Galloway Princess waiting to leave the sidings at Hove with the 08.50 Hove-Manchester Piccadilly service. When would it again see its native Scotland?
John Vaughan

Bottom:
Inside 'B' Shop at Ilford in April 1986, ex-North British Class 84 electric locomotive No 84009 is in use solely for provision of the electricity required for the conversions taking place of TSO(T) coaches to 'Choice Express' Catering RMB(T)s for use on the then forthcoming cross-London InterCity services. The locomotive's paintwork and number, ADB968021, both reflect that it is now a departmental vehicle. Brian Morrison

ADB 968021

Above:

To celebrate the 150th anniversary of the Great Western Railway, four Class 47s were repainted into GWR lined green. They were Nos 47079 *G. J. Churchward*, 47484 *Isambard Kingdom Brunel*, 47500 *Great Western* and 47628 *Sir Daniel Gooch*. On 14 September 1985 No 47484 waits to leave Paddington with the 09.15 Paddington-Hereford 'Red Dragon' Chartex. *John Vaughan*

Below:

As the last of the sub-class to be given a full classified overhaul and repaint, the opportunity was taken to put Class 33/0 No 33008 *Eastleigh* back into the closest form of original green livery that regulations now allow. On a particularly drab 6 June 1986, the locomotive leads standard Rail blue No 33031 into Clapham Junction prior to propelling the 11.08 vans train from Eastleigh into Clapham Yard. *Brian Morrison*

Left:

On the evening prior to the Network SouthEast launch, the first Class 47 to be given their distinctive colours was displayed at Liverpool Street for its official naming of *The London Standard*. Following the ceremony, No 47573 is caught by the camera just prior to returning to Stratford Traction Repair Shop for the Network SouthEast lettering to be included on the bodysides for the official 'brand name' unveiling on the following morning.   *Brian Morrison*

Below:

Class 50 'Hoover' No 50017 *Royal Oak* in Network SouthEast red, white, blue and grey heads the 15.10 Waterloo-Exeter St Davids train through Clapham cutting on 21 June 1986.   *Chris Morrison*

Top:
Although the majority of the London termini had a part to play in the Network SouthEast launch on 10 June 1986, it was at Waterloo that the main ceremony took place. To prelude events two trains were simultaneously driven into platforms 1 and 2, with Class 50 No 50023 _Howe_ on the left and an 8-car 455/8 formation consisting of sets Nos 5850 and 5872 on the right. All the stock of both trains was painted in the new Sector colours. *Brian Morrison*

Above:
In special livery for the Oban-Crianlarich summer shuttle, a BRC&W Class 104 DMU No 104325, in maroon and white livery, waits to depart Oban on 10 May 1985. *J. Reside*

Top:
Eastern Region's 'Stourton Saloon' made up of an old Gloucester RC&W Class 100 twin set, and now numbered TDB975664/975637, is pictured at Cargo Fleet, Middlesbrough, on 30 September 1985 running an officers' special from the British Steel works at Lackenby to York. The set was given this distinctive paint job at Ilford Depot where, surprisingly, the small yellow warning panel was included. *Peter J. Robinson*

Above:
A 'new generation' DMU with a new generation livery. Dressed up in the distinctive Provincial Sector colours, Class 150/1 set No 150106 runs down to the Spital Bridge stabling point at Peterborough on 6 March 1986 whilst engaged on crew training turns. *Bill Sharman*

Left:
The blue and canary yellow colours of the West Midlands PTE are carried by Class 312 EMU No 312204 on 28 September 1985 forming the 14.21 service from Birmingham New Street to Coventry. The unit is pulling away from Lea Hall station having made the required stop. *Robert Jones*

Below left:
Nicely turned out in GWR chocolate and cream in connection with the GWR150 celebrations, Pressed Steel Co 3-car DMU No B430 passes Ashton Junction on 27 May 1985 forming the 12.10 Bristol Temple Meads-Portishead special. DMS No W51410 leads. *Stephen Montgomery*

Below:
Stratford Traction Repair Shop (TRS) has long had a reputation for providing something special with its charges so far as embellishments are concerned. From making their own nameplates, to providing Union Jack bodysides for a royal wedding, to silver roofs, the staff excelled even themselves in April 1986 when they returned the oldest surviving DMU in BR service to its original green livery with front whiskers. Proudly on display outside the TRS on 11 April is the Cravens Class 105 consisting of driving trailer second (DTS) No E54122 and driving motor brake second (DMBS) No E53359. The unit went on to work the last days of a diesel service on the Southminster and Sudbury branches prior to EMUs taking over on 12 May. *Brian Morrison*

Top:
Although rather work-stained, the distinctive colours of the West Yorkshire Passenger Transport Executive still stand out on this Class 141 2-car DMU set No 141018, comprising driving motor seconds Nos 55518 and 55538. The train is the 15.40 service from Marsden to Leeds and is photographed prior to leaving Marsden on 12 March 1986.   *Larry Goddard*

Above:
A Class 303 3-car EMU set painted in the attractive red livery of Strathclyde PTE, forms an Airdrie-Helensburgh train on 29 May 1985 and passes Bowling Harbour.
Tom Noble

Above right:
Not even the old 1959 Gloucester RC&W Co Class 128 parcels vans are excused from new colours! On 4 May 1986 No M55994 poses at Tyseley dressed in 'Red Star' red, white and blue.   *Robert Jones*

Right:
The original London & South East Sector colours of brown, orange and beige were applied to a number of Southern Region Class 411/5 4-CEP EMU sets and a few of the 'Clacton Express' Class 309s of Eastern Region — and very elegant the livery looked too. The colours are likely to be retained for some time on the stock now used for the electrified Hastings services. On 23 May 1986 a 12-CEP combination, with unit No 1534 leading, speeds through Petts Wood station forming an evening '1066 Route' train from Charing Cross to Hastings. *Brian Morrison*

Class 142 2-car DMUs allocated to Plymouth Laira have been given a smart brown and cream livery for use on West Country local services and have been labelled 'Skippers'. The driver of No 142018 is about to exchange the single line token with the signalman at Crediton on 15 July 1986 whilst forming the 12.33 train from Barnstaple to Exmouth via Exeter St Davids. *Brian Morrison*

Despite being relative newcomers, the Southern Region fleet of Class 455 EMUs were all delivered in the basic blue and grey livery that became the standard for BR following the mundane 'Rail blue' which had held sway since the 1960s. Now, however, Network SouthEast red, white, blue and grey has taken over. On 21 August 1985, Class 455/7 No 5704 and Class 455/8 No 5833 approach Ashtead, Surrey, forming the 09.12 Effingham Junction-Waterloo service. The trailer seconds incorporated into the 455/7 units were originally a part of the 4-car Class 508 EMUs when they worked on Southern metals prior to going to Merseyside as 3-car sets; the different roof line on the second car being particularly noticeable here. *David Brown*

SEVEN

MISCELLANY

BRIDGES AND VIADUCTS

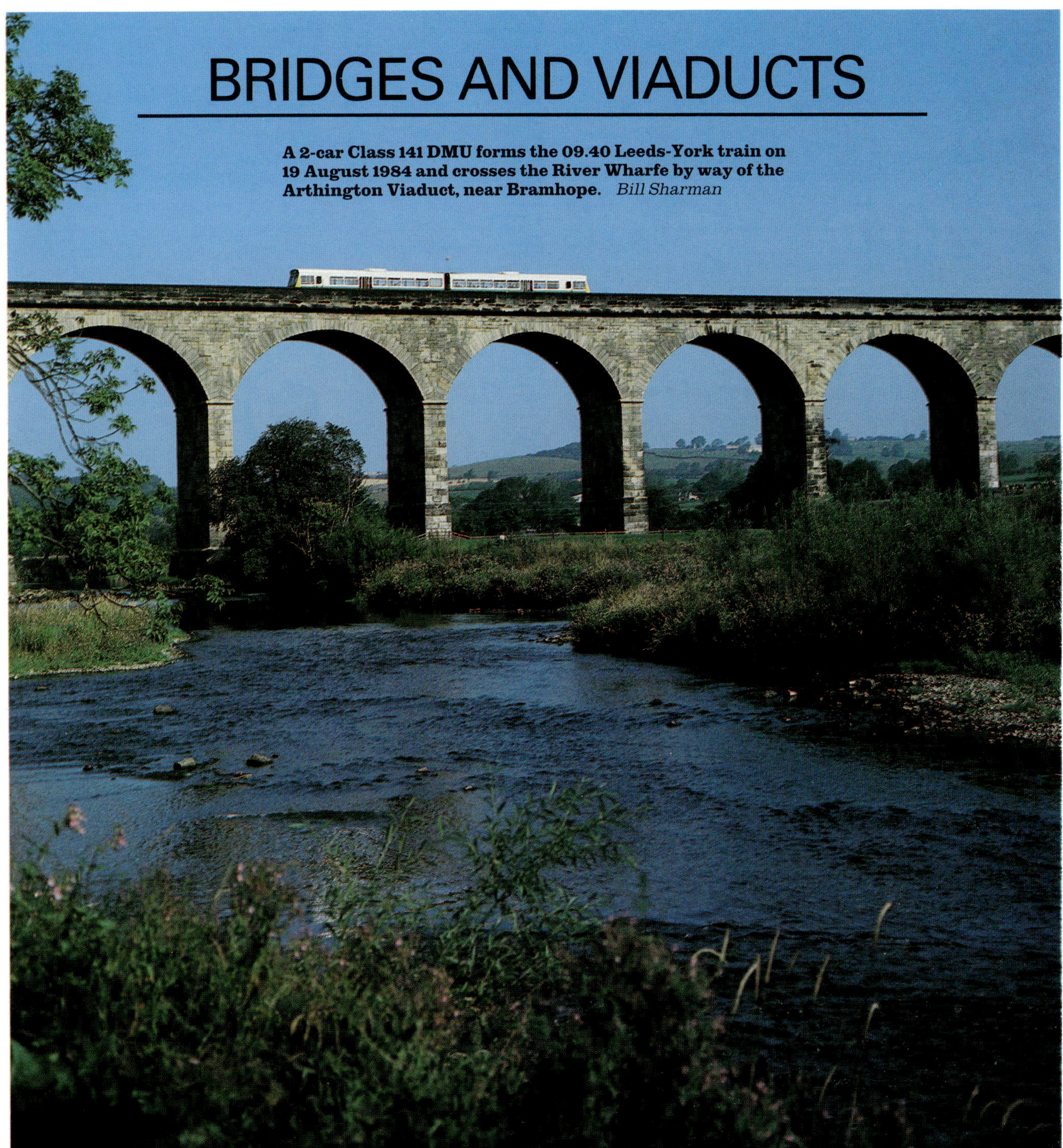

A 2-car Class 141 DMU forms the 09.40 Leeds-York train on 19 August 1984 and crosses the River Wharfe by way of the Arthington Viaduct, near Bramhope. *Bill Sharman*

Above:
The Western main line from Saltash to Penzance, in Cornwall, contains 32 substantial viaducts in its length of just over 75 miles, and the one at Coombe St Stephen, between Burngullow and Truro, is as impressive as any. On 3 October 1985, Class 50 'Hoover' No 50003 *Temeraire* **crosses with the five coaches that make up the 11.20 Penzance-Plymouth service.** *Brian Morrison*

Below:
The Kingsferry Bridge is the road and rail link from the Isle of Sheppey to the Kent mainland and is the third structure that has served the purpose since 1860. The present 270ton bridge dates from 1959; the central span is raised from the four 130ft towers, to allow craft to pass beneath, and the control room is linked to Sittingbourne signalbox as well as with the shipping traffic. On 6 September 1985, the Sittingbourne-Sheerness shuttle crosses formed of Class 411/5 4-CEP No 1563. *Brian Morrison*

THE 'GATWICK EXPRESS'

Right:
The main sphere of activity for the Class 73 electro-diesels prior to May 1984 was on a variety of freight diagrams and a few boat train workings. The decision to use them on the new 'Gatwick Express' service completely changed what had gone before and the new 15-minute interval service between London Victoria and Gatwick Airport resulted in Class 33s taking over a number of their previous duties. On the day that the services were inaugurated, No 73123, painted in InterCity livery to match the new stock, was named *Gatwick Express* and carried a special headboard to mark the occasion. *Brian Morrison*

Below:
The Class 73s, for the most part, haul the trains from Victoria and propel them from Gatwick. The stock is made up of a rake of rebuilt Mk 2 air-conditioned coaches with a Gatwick Luggage Van (GLV) rebuilt from redundant HAP motor coaches. With GLV No 9104 leading, and No 73113 bringing up the rear, an up 'Gatwick Express' passes a 4-BIG EMU heading a down Littlehampton/Portsmouth Harbour service between Clapham Junction and Wandsworth Common on the same day. *Brian Morrison*

Top:
At Borwick, near Carnforth, on 12 December 1981, a four-car Class 108 DMU formation traverses a suitably seasonal landscape as the 11.24 train from Morecambe to Leeds on 12 December 1981. *Bill Sharman*

Above:
Class 423 4-VEP EMU No 7823 hurries away from Basingstoke forming the 09.12 Bournemouth-Waterloo service, also on 12 December 1981.
Les Bertram

Right:
Working in multiple, Class 37s Nos 37200 and 37070 power a rake of tanks on the Copy Pit line in the late winter of 1981. *Graham Roose*

Right:
Heavy falls of snow in Cornwall may not be unique but they
are certainly unusual. On 19 January 1985 Class 47/4
No 47491, leaves a shivering Liskeard with the 10.50
Saturdays only Penzance-Brighton service. *John Vaughan*

Left:
The lamps on the buffer stops cast a rather strange red glow on to snowplough No ADM965228 and Class 104 trailer car No M59228 at Buxton on 21 February 1985.   *Brian Morrison*

Below left:
On the cold night of 21 February 1985, the yard lights at Buxton illuminate Class 45/0 'Peak' No 45044 and Class 20 No 20135. Both locomotives are stabled for the night having brought in earlier freight workings.   *Brian Morrison*

Above:
A pair of BRC&W Class 26/0s, Nos 26034 and 26041, await departure time at Aberdeen on the evening of 14 November 1984 with a train for Inverness.   *Colin J. Marsden*

Below:
Just one week earlier, on 7 November 1984, the same photographer is at Doncaster to record Brush Class 31/4 No 31446 heading the 21.00 to Hull.   *Colin J. Marsden*

CONSTRUCTION AND MAINTENANCE

Top:
A colourful and interesting scene at the BREL Works, Doncaster, with Class 58 No 58025 under construction on 20 November 1984.
Colin J. Marsden

Above:
On 8 May 1984, Class 87/0 No 87007 *City of Manchester* receives attention inside Willesden Depot.   *Brian Morrison*

Left:
Inside Stratford's Traction Repair Shop on 16 January 1986, two Class 37s and a variety of Class 47s receive attention for, inter alia, power unit repairs, derailment and collision damage, bogie overhaul, tyre turning and a fire alarm earth fault.   *Brian Morrison*

THE TRAVELLING POST OFFICE

Right:
**Birmingham RC&W Class 26/0 Bo-Bo No 26033 hammers
through the rock cutting at Nigg Bay, south of Aberdeen, on
29 March 1974 hauling the 15.30 Aberdeen-Perth Special
TPO. The first of the four passenger carriages which are
permitted to be conveyed with this train is just visible.**
Brian Morrison

Below:
**With the sun very low in the sky, the 19.22 Penzance-
Paddington TPO leaves the Cornish terminus behind on the
first day of May 1985 and is powered eastwards by Class 50
'Hoover' No 50005 *Collingwood*.**   *Jean Marsden*

APPENDICES

Diesel Locomotives

Class	Wheel type	Introduced	Built	Engine	Power
03	0-6-0DM	1958	BR Swindon & Doncaster	Gardner 4-cyl	204bhp
08	0-6-0DE	1953	BR Darlington, Derby, Doncaster, Crewe & Horwich	EE 6-cyl	350bhp
08/9	0-6-0DE	Rebuilt from Class 08		EE 6-cyl	350bhp
09	0-6-0DE	1959	BR	EE 6-cyl	350bhp
20	Bo-Bo	1957	English Electric	EE 8-cyl	1,000bhp
25/1	Bo-Bo	1963	BR Darlington & Derby	Sulzer 6-cyl	1,250bhp
25/2	Bo-Bo	1963	BR Darlington & Derby	Sulzer 6-cyl	1,250bhp
25/3	Bo-Bo	1966	BR Derby/Beyer Peacock	Sulzer 6-cyl	1,250bhp
25/9	Bo-Bo	Converted from Class 25/3		Sulzer 6-cyl	1,250bhp
26/0	Bo-Bo	1958	Birmingham RC&W	Sulzer 6-cyl	1,160bhp
26/1	Bo-Bo	1959	Birmingham RC&W	Sulzer 6-cyl	1,160bhp
27/0	Bo-Bo	1961	Birmingham RC&W	Sulzer 6-cyl	1,250bhp
31/1	A1A-A1A	1959	Brush Traction	EE 12-cyl	1,470bhp
31/4	A1A-A1A	Converted from Class 31/0		EE 12-cyl	1,470bhp
33/0	Bo-Bo	1960	Birmingham RC&W	Sulzer 8-cyl	1,550bhp
33/1	Bo-Bo	1960	Birmingham RC&W	Sulzer 8-cyl	1,550bhp
33/2	Bo-Bo	1962	Birmingham RC&W	Sulzer 8-cyl	1,550bhp
37/0	Co-Co	1960	English Electric	EE 12-cyl	1,750bhp
37/4	Co-Co	1985	See note	EE 12-cyl	1,750bhp
37/5	Co-Co	1986	See note	EE 12-cyl	1,750bhp
37/7	Co-Co	1986	See note	EE 12-cyl	1,750bhp
37/9	Co-Co	1986	See note	Mirrlees/Ruston	1,750bhp
40	1Co-Co1	1958	English Electric	EE 16-cyl	2,000bhp
45/0	1Co-Co1	1960	BR Derby & Crewe	Sulzer 12-cyl	2,500bhp
45/1	1Co-Co1	1960	BR Derby & Crewe	Sulzer 12-cyl	2,500bhp
47/0	Co-Co	1962	Brush/BR Crewe	Sulzer 12-cyl	2,580bhp
47/3	Co-Co	1964	Brush	Sulzer 12-cyl	2,580bhp
47/4	Co-Co	1962	Brush/BR Crewe	Sulzer 12-cyl	2,580bhp
47/7	Co-Co	1979	See note	Sulzer 12-cyl	2,580bhp
47/9	Co-Co	1979	See note	Ruston 12-cyl	3,250bhp
50	Co-Co	1967	English Electric	EE 16-cyl	2,700bhp
56	Co-Co	1977	Electroputere/BREL Doncaster & Crewe	Ruston 16-cyl	3,250bhp
58	Co-Co	1983	BREL Doncaster	Ruston 12-cyl	3,300bhp
59	Co-Co	1985	General Motors	GM 16-cyl	3,300bhp

Notes:

37/4: Rebuilt from Class 37/0
37/5: Rebuilt from Class 37/0
37/7: Rebuilt from Class 37/0
37/9: Rebuilt from Class 37/0
47/7: Rebuilt from Class 47/4
47/9: Rebuilt from Class 47/0

Electric Locomotives

Class	Wheel type	Introduced	Built	Equipment	Power
81	Bo-Bo	1960	Birmingham RC&W	AEI	3,200bhp
82	Bo-Bo	1960	Beyer Peacock	AEI	3,300bhp
83	Bo-Bo	1960	English Electric	EE	2,950bhp
85	Bo-Bo	1961	BR Doncaster	AEI	3,200bhp
86/1	Bo-Bo	Rebuilt from Class 86/0		EE/AEI	5,000bhp
86/2	Bo-Bo	Rebuilt from Class 86/0		EE	4,040bhp
86/4	Bo-Bo	Rebuilt from Classes 86/0, 86/3		EE	4,040bhp
87/0	Bo-Bo	1973	BREL Crewe	GEC	5,000bhp
87/1	Bo-Bo	1974	BREL Crewe	GEC	4,850bhp
89	Co-Co	1986	BREL Crewe	Brush	5,830bhp

Note:
Class 86/0: Introduced 1965, built BR Doncaster/English Electric

Electro-diesel Locomotives

Class	Wheel type	Introduced	Built	Engine	Power
73/0	Bo-Bo	1962	BR Eastleigh	EE 4-cyl	600bhp diesel/ 1,600bhp electric
73/1	Bo-Bo	1965	English Electric	EE 4-cyl	600bhp diesel/ 1,600bhp electric

InterCity 125 Power Cars

Class	Wheel type	Introduced	Built	Engine	Power
43	Bo-Bo	1976	BREL Crewe	Paxman 12-cyl/Mirrlees	2,250bhp

Diesel Multiple-Units

Class	Type	Introduced	Built	Engines	Vehicles in unit
100	Low density	1957	Gloucester RC&W	AEC	See note
101	Low density	1956	Metro-Cammell	Leyland	2/3
104	Low density	1957	Birmingham RC&W	Leyland	2/3
105	Low density	1956	Cravens	Leyland	2
107	Low density	1960	BR Derby	Leyland	3
108	Low density	1958	BR Derby	Leyland	2/3/4
110	Low density	1961	Birmingham RC&W	Rolls-Royce	2/3
111	Low density	1957	Metro-Cammell	Rolls-Royce	2/3
114	Low density	1956	BR Derby	Leyland	2
115	High density	1960	BR Derby	Leyland	4
116	High density	1957	BR Derby	Leyland	3
117	High density	1959	Pressed Steel	Leyland	3
118	High density	1960	Birmingham RC&W	Leyland	2/3
119	Cross-country	1958	Gloucester RC&W	Leyland	3
120	Cross-country	1957	BR Swindon	AEC	2/3
121	High density	1960	Pressed Steel	Leyland	1/2
122	High density	1958	Gloucester RC&W	AEC	1
127	High density	1959	BR Derby	Non-powered	See note
127	Parcels	Rebuilt from Class 127		Rolls-Royce	2
128	Parcels	1959	Gloucester RC&W	Leyland	1
141	Local	1983	Leyland/BREL Derby	Leyland	2
142	Local	1985	Leyland/BREL Derby	Leyland	2
143	Local	1985	W. Alexander/A. Barclay	Leyland	2
144	Local	1986	W. Alexander/BREL Derby	Leyland	2
150	Provincial	1984	BREL York	Cummins/Rolls-Royce	2/3
150/1	Provincial	1985	BREL York	Cummins	2
150/2	Provincial	1986	BREL York	Cummins	2
151	Provincial	1985	Metro-Cammell	Cummins	3
154	Provincial	Rebuilt from Class 150		Cummins	2/3
155	Provincial	1987	Leyland	Cummins	2
156	Provincial	1987	Metro-Cammell	Cummins	2

Notes:

Class 100: One vehicle only remains, formed as two-car unit with Class 105 car
Class 127: Trailer second vehicles only remain, formed within Class 116 units
Certain Class 101, 105, 116 & 120 power cars converted to operate as two-car parcels units

Diesel-Electric Multiple-Units

Class	Type	Introduced	Built	Engines	Vehicles in unit
202, 203	Main line	1957	BR Eastleigh	English Electric	6/4
204	Secondary	Rebuilt from Classes 205 & 206		English Electric	3
205	Secondary	1957	BR Eastleigh	English Electric	3
205/1	Secondary	Modified 1979 from Class 205		English Electric	3
206/1	Secondary	Modified 1986 from Class 205		English Electric	3
207	Secondary	1962	BR Eastleigh	English Electric	3
210	Outer-suburban	1981	BR Derby	Paxman/MTU	3/4

Left:

**With the massive superstructure of the Forth Bridge in the
background, Class 254 power car No 43101** *Edinburgh
International Festival* **leads the 10.00 Aberdeen-King's
Cross 'Aberdonian' express through Dalmeny on a sunny
October day in 1984.** *John Vaughan*

Electric Multiple-Units: Overhead Supply

Class	Type	Introduced	Built	Equipment	Power supply	Vehicles in unit
302	Suburban	1959	BR Doncaster & York	EE	6.25kV & 25kV ac	4
303	Suburban	1959	Pressed Steel	EE	25kV ac	3
304	Suburban	1960	BR Wolverton	AEI	25kV ac	4
305/1	Outer-suburban	1960	BR York	EE	6.25kV & 25kV ac	3
305/2	Outer-suburban	1960	BR Doncaster	EE	6.25kV & 25kV ac	4
307	Outer-suburban	1956	BR Eastleigh	EE	6.25kV & 25kV ac	4
308/1	Suburban	1961	BR York	EE	6.25kV & 25kV ac	4
308/2	Suburban	1961	BR York	EE	6.25kV & 25kV ac	3
308/3	Suburban	1961	BR York	EE	6.25kV & 25kV ac	3
309/1	Express	1962	BR York	EE	6.25kV & 25kV ac	4
309/3	Express	1962	BR York	EE	6.25kV & 25kV ac	4
309/4	Express	1962	BR York	EE	6.25kV & 25kV ac	4
310	Semi-fast	1965	BR Derby	EE	25kV ac	4
311	Suburban	1967	Cravens	AEI	25kV ac	3
312/0	Semi-fast	1977	BREL York	GEC	25kV ac	4
312/1	Semi-fast	1975	BREL York	GEC	25kV ac	4
312/2	Semi-fast	1976	BREL York	GEC	25kV ac	4
313	Suburban	1976	BREL York	GEC	25kV ac & 750V dc	3
314	Suburban	1979	BREL York	GEC/Brush	25kV ac	3
315	Suburban	1980	BREL York	GEC	25kV ac	4
317	Outer-suburban	1981	BREL Derby & York	GEC	25kV ac	3
317/2	Outer-suburban	1985	BREL Derby & York	GEC	25kV ac	3
318	Outer-suburban	1986	BREL Derby & York	GEC	25kV ac	4
319	Cross-London		BREL York		25kV ac & 750V dc	4

Note:

Class 319 to be introduced 1987

**In Network SouthEast livery, a BR Derby Class 310 EMU,
looking very sprightly despite its 25 years, works a special
train from Euston on 10 June 1986.** *Brian Morrison*

Electric Multiple-Units: Third Rail

Class	Type	Introduced	Built	Equipment	Power supply	Vehicles in unit
411/3 (4-CEP)	Express	1958	BR Eastleigh	EE	750V dc	4
411/4 (4-CEP)	Express	1956	BR Eastleigh	EE	750V dc	4
411/5 (4-CEP)	Express	1958	BR Eastleigh	EE	750V dc	4
412/3 (4-BEP)	Express	1956	BR Eastleigh	EE	750V dc	4
413/2 (4-CAP)	Secondary	1957	BR Eastleigh	EE	750V dc	4
413/3 (4-CAP)	Secondary	1958	BR Eastleigh	EE	750V dc	4
414/2 (2-HAP)	Secondary	1957	BR Eastleigh	EE	750V dc	2
414/3 (2-HAP)	Secondary	1958	BR Eastleigh	EE	750V dc	2
415/1 (4-EPB)	Suburban	1951	BR Eastleigh	EE	750V dc	4
415/3 (4-EPB)	Suburban	1960	BR Eastleigh	EE	750V dc	4
415/4 (4-EPB)	Suburban	1951	BR Eastleigh	EE	750V dc	4
415/6 (4-EPB)	Suburban	1960	BR Eastleigh	EE	750V dc	4
416/2 (2-EPB)	Suburban	1953	BR Eastleigh	EE	750V dc	2
416/3 (2-EPB)	Suburban	1953	BR Eastleigh	EE	750V dc	2
416/4 (2-EPB)	Suburban	1953	BR Eastleigh	EE	750V dc	2
419 (MLV)	Luggage van	1959	BR Eastleigh	EE	750V dc	1
421/1 (4-CIG)	Express	1964	BR York	EE	750V dc	4
421/2 (4-CIG)	Express	1970	BREL York	EE	750V dc	4
421/3 (4-CIG)	Express	1964	BR York	EE	750V dc	4
421/4 (4-CIG)	Express	1970	BREL York	EE	750V dc	4
422/1 (4-BIG)	Express	1965	BR York	EE	750V dc	4
422/2 (4-BIG)	Express	1970	BREL York	EE	750V dc	4
423 (4-VEP)	Express	1967	BR/BREL York	EE	750V dc	4
432 (4-REP)	Express	1967	BR/BREL York	EE	750V dc	4
438 (4-TC)	Express trailer	1966	BR/BREL York			4
455/7	Suburban	1984	BREL York	GEC/Brush	750V dc	4
455/8	Suburban	1982	BREL York	GEC	750V dc	4
455/9	Suburban	1985	BREL York	GEC	750V dc	4
485 (5-VEC)	Isle of Wight	1967	Metro-Cammell/ Union Car Co/ Cammell Laird	BTH	630V dc	5
486 (2-TIS)	Isle of Wight	1967	Metro-Cammell/ Union Car Co/ Cammell Laird	BTH	630V dc	2
487	Waterloo & City	1940	English Electric	EE	600V dc	2/5
488/2	'Gatwick Express'	1983	BREL Derby			2
488/3	'Gatwick Express'	1983	BREL Derby			3
489	Driving luggage van	1983	BREL Eastleigh	EE	750V dc	1
504	Suburban	1959	BR Wolverton	EE	1,200V dc	2
507	Suburban	1978	BREL York	GEC	750V dc	3
508	Suburban	1979	BREL York	GEC	750V dc	3

Notes:

411/3 & 411/5: Converted from Class 411/2, refurbished, 1975 & 1979
411/4: Converted from Class 411/1, refurbished, 1980
412/3: Converted from Class 410, refurbished, 1982
413/2 & 413/3: Formed of two former Class 414 two-car units (built 1956), 1982
415/4: Converted from Class 415/1, refurbished, 1978
415/6: Converted from Class 415/3, refurbished, 1983
416/3: Converted from Class 416/1, refurbished, 1983
416/4: Converted from Class 416/2, refurbished, 1985
421/3: Converted from Class 421/1 and Class 420/1, refurbished, 1985
421/4: Converted from Class 421/2, refurbished, 1986
422/1: Converted from Class 420/1, refurbished, 1985
422/2: Converted from Class 420/2, refurbished, 1985
438: Formerly Class 491
455/7: Includes former Class 508 trailer second
485 & 486: Converted from former London Transport underground stock, built 1923-1935
488/2 & 488/3: Converted from standard Mk 2f stock
489: Rebuilt from Class 414 motor brake second for 'Gatwick Express' service

The tables on pages 91-95 detail the BR fleet as at December 1986.

The much-loved 'Deltics' were the most powerful passenger diesel locomotives on BR, at 3,300bhp, and for almost 20 years dominated East Coast main line passenger services. No 55013 *The Black Watch* powers up Beattock Bank with a diverted King's Cross-Edinburgh train on 4 May 1980. *D. Rogers*